Exploring Citizenship

Honesty

Sue Barraclough

Heinemann Library,
Chicago, IL

www.heinemannraintree.com
Visit our website to find out
more information about
Heinemann-Raintree books.

To order:
☎ Phone 888-454-2279
💻 Visit www.heinemannraintree.com
to browse our catalog and order online.

©2010 Heinemann Library
an imprint of Capstone Global Library, LLC
Chicago, Illinois

Edited by Rebecca Rissman and Catherine Veitch
Designed by Ryan Frieson and Betsy Wernert
Picture research by Elizabeth Alexander and
Rebecca Sodergren
Production by Duncan Gilbert
Originated by Heinemann Library
Printed in China by South China Printing Company Ltd

Library of Congress Cataloging-in-Publication Data

Barraclough, Sue.
  Honesty / Sue Barraclough.
    p. cm. -- (Exploring citizenship)
  Includes bibliographical references and index.
   ISBN 978-1-4329-3311-1 (hc) -- ISBN 978-1-4329-3319-7 (pb) 1.
  Honesty--Juvenile literature. 2. Citizenship--Juvenile literature. I.
  Title.
  BJ1533.H7B37 2008
  179'.9--dc22

                         2008055297

Acknowledgments

We would like to thank the following for permission to reproduce
photographs: Alamy **pp. 5** (© David R. Frazier Photolibrary, Inc.),
7 (© Feel Images), **8** (© Ian Shaw), **11** (© SELF) **17** (© Angela
Hampton Picture Library), **19** (© UpperCut Images/Rachel Weill),
23 (© Big Cheese Photo LLC); Corbis **pp. 6** (© John Madere),
13 (© Randy Faris), **12** (© Jose Luis Pelaez, Inc.), **22** (© H&S
Produktion), **24** (© Steve Cole/Anyone/amanaimages), **25**
(© Heide Benser), **27** (© Roy McMahon); Getty Images **pp. 4**
(Lena Granefelt/Johner Images), **9** (Louis Fox/Stone), **15** (John
Howard/Stone), **16** (Eg Project/Photonica), **18** (Seiya Kawamoto/
Taxi), **20** (Tara Moore/Taxi), **26** (Simone Mueller/Taxi), **29** (Simon
Watson/Stone); Photolibrary **p. 10** (Heidi Vetten/Mauritius).

Cover photograph of a girl cheating reproduced with permission of
Getty Images (Nicole Hill/Rubberball Productions).

The publishers would like to thank Yael Biederman for her help in
the preparation of this book.

Every effort has been made to contact copyright holders of any
material reproduced in this book. Any omissions will be rectified
in subsequent printings if notice is given to
the publisher.

Contents

Some words are shown in bold, **like this**. You can find out what they mean by looking in the glossary.

What Is Citizenship?

Citizenship is about being a member of a group. A group is a family, a school, a team, or a country. Citizenship is about having certain **rights** and **responsibilities**.

Your family is a group you probably spend a lot of time with.

At school everyone needs to behave in certain ways to keep everyone safe and happy.

Having rights means there are certain ways that other people should treat you. Having responsibilities means you should act or behave in a certain way. As a member of a family or a member of a school, there are right and wrong ways to behave.

What Is Honesty?

Honesty is telling the truth. The truth means **facts** about a person or something that has happened.

You always feel better when you tell the truth.

Honesty is saying what you think happened as clearly as you can. If you are not sure what happened, then it is honest to say so.

Honesty is also being open about how you feel.

Honest Behavior

Good friends are honest with each other.

Honest behavior is about being **reliable** and doing what you say you will. You are honest when you keep promises.

A promise is saying you will definitely do something. Keeping a promise is doing what you say you will. For example, you might promise to lend a toy to a friend or sit next to a friend in class.

If a friend did not keep a promise or told a lie, how would that make you feel?

Honesty and Truth

It is important to be honest, even if it is difficult to tell the truth. Telling the truth can sometimes hurt a friend's feelings, but it is important to always try to tell the truth.

Good friends know they can tell each other the truth without meaning to hurt each other.

How do you feel
when someone is not
honest with you?

It is easier to be friends with people if you
know they are honest. If you are not sure
a friend is honest, it might make you feel
unhappy and worried. You will not be able
to **trust** the friend.

It Was Not Me!

A lie is when you choose to say something that is not true. Telling lies is not a good thing, even when it is hard to tell the truth.

Often when you lie, people find out that you have not told the truth.

Imagine you broke or damaged something. You might want to tell a lie so you or a friend will not be in trouble. Even if you might get into trouble, it is important not to lie.

When things get damaged or broken, it is always best to tell the truth.

13

Truth and Trust

Telling a lie can sometimes seem like a good idea. But it is important to think about what might happen if you tell a lie. Think about how it will make you and other people feel.

If you tell a lie:

- ☑ You will worry that someone will find out.
- ☑ Other people will not trust you if they find out.
- ☑ Even if no one finds out, you know you have lied and you will feel bad.
- ☑ If someone else gets the blame, you will feel bad.

It feels good to be respected and trusted.

If you tell a lie and you are found out, you will lose **trust**. If you tell the truth you may still be in trouble, but you earn **respect** and trust for being honest. If you trust someone, you are sure they are honest and will choose to do the right thing.

Lost and Found

Sometimes people drop things or leave them behind. If you find something, what do you think is the right thing to do? Do you think you have a **right** to keep something when you find it?

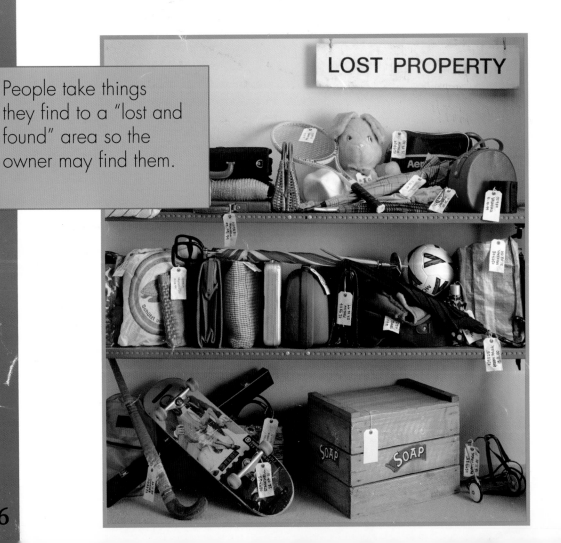

People take things they find to a "lost and found" area so the owner may find them.

LOST PROPERTY

Always think about how the owner must feel if you find something that is lost.

Think about it

How do you feel when you have lost something? Do you feel happy that you have lost it, or do you want it back?

If you find something that someone has lost, move it to an obvious place where it could be found. Or give it to an adult to deal with.

Respect for Property

It is important to **respect** other people's **property**. To show your respect, you can do the following things:
- Ask to use or borrow things.
- Do not just take something.
- Be careful with things you have borrowed.
- Ask an adult what to do if you find lost property.

Always treat other people's things as if they are your own.

Leave adults' wallets alone unless you have permission to touch them.

Sometimes it is **tempting** to take money. If you find money that looks as if it does not belong to anyone, it is still not right to take it. The best **rule** is that if it is not yours, leave it where it is.

What Is Cheating?

People may cheat or bend the rules because they want to do well or win.

When you are learning to play a game or sport, you learn the **rules**. Rules make games and sports **fair** for everyone. When people cheat they choose not to play by the rules.

Sometimes you may feel you want to win so badly that you think that winning is all that matters. It is important to think about what might happen if you cheat.

If you cheat to win:

☑ Will you feel that you have done well?

☑ Do you think you will feel proud of yourself?

☑ Will it make you feel bad that you have not won fairly?

☑ Will you feel sad that you have cheated?

Copying

Copying is a type of cheating that sometimes happens in school. For example, a friend may try to look at your answers when you have been told to work on your own.

It can be difficult if a friend tries to copy your work.

When friends cheat, you may have different feelings. You may want to help them or you may feel angry that they are copying your work. It is better to cover your answers, so your friends cannot cheat.

If you copy other people's work, you do not learn for yourself.

Tattling

Talking about problems with friends will help you to be honest.

Sometimes you may feel that you are tattling by being honest. But it is important to be honest with yourself and others about things that you think are wrong.

When you tell an adult about something bad that has happened, you may be helping other people to stay safe.

If you see something happening, such as bullying or unkind behavior, it is important to tell an adult or a teacher. This is not tattling, it is doing the right thing.

Is Honesty Important?

You need to be able to **trust** your friends and family to be honest so that everyone can live happily together.

Imagine what it would be like if you could not trust your parents, your teachers, or your friends to be honest.

Would you be happy if you knew your friends could not trust you?

If you tell a lie or do something **dishonest**, other people may not find out. But even if they do not find out, you will know.

Honesty and Happiness

It is important to be honest so that people will **trust** you and you will feel good about yourself.

Honesty is:

- ☑ telling the truth
- ☑ keeping promises
- ☑ doing what you say you will
- ☑ **respecting** other people's **property**
- ☑ asking when you want to borrow or use things
- ☑ following **rules**
- ☑ admitting to mistakes and saying "sorry"
- ☑ taking **responsibility** and not blaming others.

Being honest in the way you think, speak, and behave is good for friendships. Honesty makes the world a happier, safer place.

Everyone feels happier with good friends.

Glossary

dishonest being untruthful. Lying to someone is being dishonest.

fact something that is true or has happened

fair way of behaving that treats everyone equally and that everyone is happy with

property something that belongs to you

reliable trusted to behave well

respect way of treating someone or something with kindness and politeness

responsibility something that it is your job to do as a good and helpful member of a group

right how you should be treated by others, in a way that is thought to be good or fair by most people

rule something that says how things should be done, and tells you what you are allowed or not allowed to do

tempt make someone want to do something, often something that is wrong or not honest

trust know someone is good and honest

Find Out More

Books

Loewen, Nancy. *How Could You?: Kids Talk About Trust.* Mankato, Minn.: Picture Window, 2003.

Mayer, Cassie. *Being Honest.* Chicago: Heinemann Library, 2008.

Mayer, Cassie. *Being Responsible.* Chicago: Heinemann Library, 2008.

Nettleton, Pamela Hill. *Is That True?: Kids Talk About Honesty.* Mankato, Minn.: Picture Window, 2005.

Small, Mary. *Being a Good Citizen: A Book About Citizenship.* Mankato, Minn.: Picture Window, 2006.

Website

www.hud.gov/kids

This government Website shows children what it means to be good citizens.

Index